24/

TIMELESS
TREASURES

TIMELESS TREASURES

Inspired Ideas for Decorating Your Home

Lauren Powell

Sterling Publishing Co., Inc.
New York

PROLIFIC IMPRESSIONS PRODUCTION STAFF:

Editor in Chief: Mickey Baskett
Copy Editor: Phyllis Mueller
Graphics: Dianne Miller, Karen Turpin
Styling: Kirsten Jones
Photography: Jerry Mucklow, David Bjurstrom
Administration: Jim Baskett

Library of Congress Cataloging-in-Publication Data

Powell, Lauren
    Timeless treasures : inspired ideas for decorating your home / Lauren Powell.
        p. cm.
    Includes index.
    ISBN 0-8069-6885-0
        1. Collectibles in interior decoration. I. Title.

    NK2115.5.C58 P692 2002
    747--dc21

                                                                                2002030398

10 9 8 7 6 5 4 3 2 1

Published by Sterling Publishing Co., Inc.
387 Park Avenue South, New York, N.Y. 10016

© Copyright 2003 by Prolific Impressions, Inc.
Produced by Prolific Impressions, Inc.
160 South Candler St., Decatur, GA 30030

Distributed in Canada by Sterling Publishing
c/o Canadian Manda Group, One Atlantic Avenue, Suite 105
Toronto, Ontario, Canada M6K 3E7
Distributed in Great Britain by Chrysalis Books
64 Brewery Road, London N7 9NT, England
Distributed in Australia by Capricorn Link (Australia) Pty. Ltd.
P.O. Box 704, Winsor, NSW 2756 Australia

Printed in China
All rights reserved
Sterling ISBN 0-8069-6885-0

ACKNOWLEDGEMENTS

Old Edna says, "Well...La de Da!"
Crossroads of Hwy. 227 and Price
Canyon Rd.
San Luis Obispo, California 93401
805-544-8062
www.ladedaonline.com
A treasure trove of wonderfully old furniture pieces and home decorating accents.

Ron's Nursery
1207 S. 13th Street
Grover Beach, California 93433
805-489-4747
www.ronsnursery.com
For plants and flowers for Edna's Cottage; styling by Pam Langfeldt

Walnut Hollow Farm, Inc.
1409 State Rd. 23
Dodgeville, WI 53533
800-950-5101
www.walnuthollow.com
For wooden stool, shelf, frames, and other unfinished wood items for the projects.

Houston Art, Inc.
10770 Moss Ridge Rd.
Houston, TX 77043-1175
800-272-3804
www.houstonart.com
For gold and silver leaf products

Plaid Enterprises, Inc.
P.O. Box 7600
Norcross, Georgia 30092
800-842-4197
www.plaidonline.com
For FolkArt® Acrylic Paints and Crackle Medium, Decorator Glaze, Apple Barrel Colors® Gloss Enamel Paint, Treasure Gold®

Wisconsin Lighting, Inc.
800 Wisconsin Street, Ste. D02-104
Eau Claire, WI 54703
800-657-6999
www.wilighting.com
For self-adhesive lampshade

About the Author
LAUREN POWELL

Lauren Powell's background in art and design led to her interest in home decorating and her love of collecting. Working for Plaid Enterprises, Inc., the leading arts and crafts manufacturer in the world, for over 15 years has created many opportunities for Lauren to gain product knowledge from leading designers.

Lauren is author of two other books on this subject, *Tattered Treasures*, 2001; and *Tattered Treasures for the Garden*, 2002.

She has discovered many ways to update and add artistic touches to flea market finds through painted finishes, decoupage, mosaics, and more. Her home has been featured in *Woman's Day* and *Romantic Homes* magazines as well as *The Kitty Bartholomew Show* on HGTV. Lauren has been a guest on numerous television shows, including *The Christopher Lowell Show* on the Discovery Channel.

Lauren makes her home in Austin, Texas with her husband and two children. She enjoys Bible studies and spending time with her family and her horse, Patrick. She is grateful for the opportunities she has to share her talents and help others find theirs.

Miller Photography, St. Simons Island, GA

DEDICATION

I would like to dedicate this book to my family. Without their loving support, I would not be able to take pleasure doing what I enjoy so much. They patiently watch me dig around flea markets for the perfect treasure and tolerate lots of projects in the works, all over the house! Thank you for allowing me to enjoy expressing the creativity that God has blessed me with.

A SPECIAL THANKS

I would like to thank all of the homeowners who so graciously allowed us to come in and photograph their outstanding havens to share with others. It was a pleasure to get to know so many talented and special people. Each location and experience was uniquely different and charming. Thank you to all of the following for your hospitality and friendship:

Special thanks to Eileen Paulin, editor of *Romantic Homes* magazine, for introducing me to her talented friends at Old Edna says, "Well...La de Da!" and for her contribution to the "Mellow Patina of Aging" chapter.

Judy Watkins and Pattea Torrence, owners of *Old Edna says, "Well...La de Da!"* in San Luis Obispo, California, hosted us for several days and intrigued us with their delightful shop filled with wonderful displays of new and vintage merchandise. Judy and Pattea not only escorted us to photograph their homes, but also introduced us to the spectacular homes of Patti and Steve Rarig and Sandy and Ed Howe.

Ann and Mark Rogers' personal interpretation of New England style is something to behold. Their home is a beautiful montage of authentic dark wood antiques lightened by numerous collections of magnificent china and ironware. Of special note are their teapot collection, floral china plates showcasing colors of the garden, and the use of blue and white in the nautical bedroom.

Nancy and Guy Carter's cottage in St. Simons Island, Georgia overflows with lovely collections and whimsical touches. Nancy's blue and white porcelain and her talent for display encouraged me to rearrange my own cupboards and showcase items previously tucked away. The Carters' southern hospitality and kindness will always be treasured.

Margaret Garner and Betty Sibley of Beau Maison on St. Simons Island, Georgia assisted their client Jane Calloway in creating an eclectic, one-of-a-kind seaside retreat that we all enjoyed. Jane truly appreciates the beauty of timeworn treasures, and her home is filled with distressed pieces, architectural details, and vivid colors.

Cherry Jackson's cottage lifestyle is portrayed throughout her California home. The cozily cluttered combination of fabrics, weathered wooden accents, and country kitchen decor works beautifully to create a warm and inviting refuge.

CONTENTS

The question is "where" as well as "how" when it comes to starting a collection for your home. Many of us have old things or family heirlooms. But many times we don't know how to build upon that collection or where to go to find help for enhancing our home with well used treasures.

Flea markets may seem a likely place to start. But sometimes flea markets only succeed in

age and dried flowers (much like the smell of my mother's attic), I couldn't help but feel transported to a more simple time and feel at peace with my world. It is no wonder that we began taking photos immediately for this book so that we could share their stylish look with you.

Not only were many of the photos in this book taken at this shop, but we discovered that the two

How & Where Do I Start Collecting?

confusing me. There is so much "stuff" and so many styles of things – I simply loose my vision for how I want to decorate my home. For those of you who have had this same kind of experience, I recommend finding a shop that specializes in used collectibles and has the "look" you want to achieve. They can guide you and help you keep on track for the look you want. They can also find special items for your needs through their many sources.

If you are very, very lucky, you may find a magical shop – like I did when I was introduced to *Old Edna Says, "Well...La de Da!"* located in central California. I saw a certain style and creativity in this shop that was brimming with furniture and home accessories. There was beauty at every turn – rescued furniture pieces with elegant woodworking, a gorgeous enameled clock, a piece of cut crystal, flowers everywhere filling French urns and Victorian vases. I touched wonderful textures of old leather, wood worn smooth from use, soft antique fabrics. As I walked around on the creaking old wood floors and inhaled the heady fragrance of

shop owners, Judy and Pattea also had charming homes that they have decorated with some of their finds. They have combined their collectable treasures with new fabrics and a modern sensibility to create very livable environments for their families. So we also invaded their homes.

Judy and Pattea then led me to homes of several of their customers who rely on the shop for finding just the right pieces to decorate their homes. These wonderful folks were so kind to allow us to photograph the sanctuaries they have created with their collections and finds. As you will see, each look is different and personal. They have all used old pieces creatively and their homes truly speak of the spirit of the owners. We hope you will enjoy seeing how used collectibles can add charm and warmth to a home.

Mickey Baskett

Mickey Baskett, editor

The homes photographed for this book are each unique and different, but they have a lot in common. Each is a personal reflection of the homeowners' love of tattered treasures, their one-of-a-kind finds, and individual decorating styles. Although the styles varied, we found color palettes and themes were repeated. In this book, we explore ways to decorate using favorite colors with an emphasis on found objects, collections, and do-it-yourself projects.

Color affects our moods, the way we feel, and how we act. We are each uniquely drawn to certain colors – colors that make us feel good when we are surrounded by them. From warm whites to cool blues, radiant reds to majestic metallics, the intensity or softness of a favorite color varies greatly depending on the other colors and objects that are used with it. The combination of color and nostalgia in the items used to decorate creates the styles represented in this book.

For me, the enjoyable part of decorating with flea market finds and collections is the confidence and freedom that comes from knowing that perfection is not the goal. Old items with signs of wear and age add instant warmth and comfort to a home. Imperfections are sought-after, and decorating with chipped or weathered finds is desirable. Don't worry about nicks, dents, scratches, and bumps – they only add to the well-loved appearance of older items and reflect your (and their!) individuality. Old, well-loved items hold memories and are, therefore, personal. Why not surround yourself with items from years past that will evoke recollections of special times or occasions?

The many beautiful homes featured throughout this book offer inspiring ideas that can be applied to special rooms in your own home. Use them to make your home a haven you enjoy sharing with others.

After you have enjoyed the thrill of the hunt and accumulated a variety of items you find interesting, display them and use them to individualize your home. Throughout the pages of this book, notice how the collections have been displayed. Use the ideas you see to help you show off your wonderful finds.

Shelves, cupboards, and tabletops are obvious

your collections. A wall with just framed pictures or art can be made much more interesting with the addition of an unusual object or a grouping of your collections. Displaying plates adds wonderful color and a break from the usual rectangles of framed pieces. When hanging plates on the wall, select a large plate as the focal point and work outward from there. Vary the sizes and shapes of items to

Displaying Your Collections

and appropriate places for showcasing your prized possessions; however, don't overlook the tops of armoires and cabinets or even the floor for interesting visual displays. Group items casually, without worrying too much about symmetry. Try clustering similar items together, gathering them by theme or by color – a single piece doesn't have the impact that a grouping will. Use fabric-covered boxes or architectural antiques to give height and interest to tabletop arrangements. Stacks of books, lying on their sides, can become risers for showcasing special finds. They are great for elevating small vases, clocks, statues, china plates on a stand, or picture frames. An open book is nice on a side table, with antique eyeglasses or a fancy bookmark displayed on top.

Don't disregard your walls for a place to display

create movement and interest.

Collect picture frames and display favorite photos in unexpected places. Hang a frame on the front of a bookcase or the side of a plain cabinet. Create a gallery by grouping framed pictures or mirrors on a wall.

Be creative and find many unusual ways to show and use your pieces. Use small lamps to accent collections on tabletops, and place them under wall cabinets or in bookcases to illuminate the details of intricate pieces. Prop and layer flat items like mirrors, pictures, and plates against each other for dimensional effect on a wall, shelf, or mantel. Fill old bowls and pottery with seashells, marbles, and other small collections.

Most of all, have fun with the art of display. Don't be afraid to mix textures and materials, the formal with the informal, and the new with the old.

ABOVE: *Layers of found objects are casually arranged and propped on a mantel. The mirror makes the most of three-dimensional objects like the concrete garden statue, affording a view of more than one side. A vintage tablecloth softens the hard edge of the mantelpiece. Branches in a white pitcher bring springtime indoors.*

OPPOSITE PAGE: *A kitchen cabinet displays a lovely collection of brown transferware. Stacked plates and cups mingle with larger pieces on stands to make an interesting display.*

WHITE

White makes a room appear larger when used predominantly, and it provides a clean backdrop for special collections. White rooms are soothing, restful, and relaxing, illustrating the maxim that a room can be interesting without being filled with color. The simplicity and variety of white tones work nicely with many decorating styles.

The color white varies greatly depending on its undertone or hue. Tints or shades of white may be warm or cool. Yellow undertones or hues tend to be warm, while blues are cooler and more formal. The soft brown tones found in antiqued white and weathered furniture are timeless and add warm, romantic touches. The multiple shades and gradations of color can be used together.

White accessories such as vintage creamware and white china allow the eye to enjoy the beautiful shapes without the distraction of color and pattern. Decorative and functional, white china looks beautiful displayed in a wooden cabinet. Regardless of the shade of white you select, adding texture with accessories such as pillows, quilts, throws, and rugs brings interest and individuality to a room. Soft accessories turn a stark white room into a calm and soothing haven.

RIGHT: *A collection of white enamel pitchers, creamware, and white china plates and soup tureens stand out against the country pine back of this cabinet.*

White paint can transform heavy-looking wooden dressers, armoires, and chests, bringing lightness and accenting interesting shapes. Left crisp white or mellowed with antiquing techniques, painted furniture has the ability to dramatically transform a room. Garage sales, flea markets, and salvage stores are good places to find old wooden furniture pieces just waiting for a facelift.

It's easy to re-create the look of wear and weather with paint. Choose an acrylic wall paint in an eggshell or satin sheen. Simply apply, let dry, and use sandpaper to remove some of the paint from raised details and along edges where the finish would naturally show wear over time. The eggshell or satin finish paint provides a perfect surface for applying antiquing glaze to add additional age and warmth.

LEFT: *This chest is used as a sideboard and becomes the focal point of the dining room. The intricate carved wood details are made more apparent by the white painted finish.*

When old furniture pieces are reupholstered in crisp white or natural-colored fabrics, the lines of the piece are more apparent, and if the piece has a carved wooden frame or trim, the elaborate look of the wood creates an interesting contrast with simple white fabric. Using feather or down cushions gives a soft, cozy look and feel. One caveat: White fabric can be hard to keep clean and new-looking in an active household, especially one with pets or children. One option is to apply a fabric protector – ask your upholsterer for recommendations.

To completely change the look of upholstered furniture pieces, try slipcovering them in white. Ready-made slipcovers are often available in heavy cotton duck or twill fabrics in natural or white tones. In a home with lots of activity, small children, or pets, slipcovers are a great option as they can be tossed into the wash as needed for quick cleanup.

ABOVE: *A Louis XVI sofa takes on a new look when reupholstered in white.*

RIGHT: *White backgrounds provide a clean palette for dramatic accessories – solid-color walls, floors, and furniture allow special pieces to stand out. Here, an arched iron grille mounted above the French doors becomes an ornamental focal point in this all white living room. The curves of the wall piece are echoed in the metal legs of the table nearby.*

LEFT: *Gently gathered fabrics create a dreamy environment in this all-white bedroom. The panel behind the bed is actually an antique lace tablecloth. Framed vintage prints and needlepoint pillows supply soft touches of color. The slipcovered chair provides a place for reading and relaxing; its subtle print fabric is restful and calming.*

19

LEFT: *The mirrored door of this painted armoire reflects the pretty white bedroom and houses extra bed linens. Extra pillows are casually stored on top. A drawer at the bottom showcases a collection of vintage lace.*

ABOVE: *White in a bathroom is simple, yet elegant. Wall-mounted lamps with white shades are unexpected but practical. An antique wooden frame – painted, of course, in white – holds the mirror over the sink.*

Accessories add an important decorative layer to any room. In white rooms, accessories help define and extend the mood, theme, or style. Accessory choices are endless; some of my favorites are photographs of family and friends in old wooden or iron frames.

Picture frames can be displayed on tabletops or hung, gallery fashion, on walls. Small mirrors and oil paintings are beautiful propped up on easels; large ones look interesting hung in groups of varying sizes and shapes. Architectural details such as old window frames, iron gates, columns, and wooden moldings are unique and dramatic, whether hung on the wall, arranged on tabletops, or stacked on the floor.

Fabric pillows, quilts, and throws offer colorful options. Baskets and watering cans can hold papers, magazines, flowers, or plants. Plants also naturally soften and warm a room. Try draping ivy from favorite flea market containers for a decorator look. Lamps and candles add a soft, warm glow and sweet scents to a room.

Think creatively and make new and unusual accessories from parts and pieces of others. An old frame, for example, might become a shadow box for displaying favorite collectibles or could surround a mirror. Old columns can hold plants. An iron gate can be a tabletop. Don't be afraid to invent your own imaginative creations.

RIGHT: *An old iron gate was attached to four salvaged balusters and topped with glass for a one-of-a-kind coffee table.*

LEFT: *The use of color – in a hooked rug with a floral border, fresh flowers, and a painting of flowers in a vintage frame – is restrained in this white bedroom. A mismatched pair of lamps with similar white shades flank the bed. A collection of pillows in vintage fabrics is soft and inviting on the bed.*

BELOW: *Layering and stacking large and small items on a bedside table add interest and movement. Lamplight sheds a warm glow.*

ABOVE: *United by color, a gathering of objects can become a collection. A weathered shelf with dentil molding mounted above a contemporary fireplace serves as a mantel. Topped with an artful arrangement that includes creamware pitchers, bottles, turned wood pieces, a lamp, and a framed picture, it becomes a decorative focal point. The piece of iron fence, placed over the opening, is an unusual fire screen. Fireplace tools are gathered in an old umbrella stand. Interesting architectural fragments are piled on the hearth.*

RIGHT: *A classic garden decoration, the large birdhouse guides the eye upward atop a painted armoire. Color is supplied by green plants and a green wicker table.*

27

Storage is essential in any room. Old furniture, freshly painted, offers a clean and perfect solution for common storage problems in dining rooms, kitchens, and bathrooms. Lined drawers can be filled with linens and silverware, while larger compartments hold trays and serving bowls.

Open shelves can house cookbooks and display dishes. Towels stacked by size and color could fill an old cupboard or armoire in the bathroom. Storage pieces also provide an additional surfaces for serving food or displaying special collections.

LEFT: *A vintage cabinet stores baskets, china, and placemats. Potted plants, gathered in a wooden planter reach for the light from the window.*

OPPOSITE PAGE: *A 19th century oval wooden table, painted white, is a colorful island in this homey kitchen. When not in use during cooking, the table becomes a nice display area with the addition of a watering can filled with fresh flowers. The table's curves are a pleasant contrast in a room of straight lines and hard surfaces.*

ABOVE: *The individual compartments of an old mail sorting cabinet salvaged from a post office display an assortment of small collectibles. It sits atop an old chest.*

RIGHT: *A painted white buffet with classical motif trim is ready for a party. Parfait glasses hold silverware; a toast rack displays a assortment of folded cloth napkins. A plate on a marble pedestal carries a seashell collection.*

31

Painted beadboard wainscoting invokes the charm of cottage life and adds subtle vertical lines to the walls. Sold in sheets, it's an easy way to give a casual country look to a room. Simply cut to size, nail to the wall, and paint.

Here, *at left,* the wainscoting lends an old-timey look to a cozy breakfast nook in the kitchen and creates the perfect background for a mix of old and new furnishings. One would never guess that it hasn't been there for years.

BELOW: *Graceful, interesting shapes, united by color, create an eye-catching tabletop display of old china. Pictured is a cheese cover, salt & pepper set, porcelain coffee pot, cream pitcher, and a miniature cream pitcher.*

Lace panels draped over a pair of French doors, *below,* softly filter the sunshine. A vintage dressing gown, hung from a coat hanger on the door molding, becomes part of the window treatment. The soft window coverings and curvy upholstered furniture balance the angular marble fireplace and framed mirror. The iron firescreen adds additional texture and interest.

In a living room full of white upholstered furniture, the natural wood
of a pine armoire, *above,* stands out. Cascades of dried flowers pick up
the tone of the wood.

ABOVE: *Beautifully tied ribbon embellished with berries cleverly binds a stack of linens at the foot of the bed on an old cane chair.*

RIGHT: *Sunshine fills the room, filtered through the delicate cutwork and lace of a vintage tablecloth that is draped over a curtain rod. A silk rose and tassel are stitched in place at the center to form a swag.*

Whether used in a kitchen, dining room, or beside a bed, aged wooden tables blend beautifully with the neutral shades of white. The French table, pictured below and at right, was painted white and antiqued. The mellow look is a gentle background for vintage table linens and china. A mismatched collection of chairs shows how versatile this type of table can be.

MAKE-IT-YOURSELF

How to Create an Aged Finish

SUPPLIES

Unfinished wooden item

Acrylic craft paints - Raw umber and
warm white or other topcoat
(soft green is good, too!)

Petroleum jelly

Sponge brush

Bristle brush

Wood-tone antiquing glaze

Sandpaper - Medium grade

Soft paper towels

INSTRUCTIONS

1. Mix 1 part raw umber paint with 3 parts water to make a stain. Using the sponge brush, apply the stain to the surface, brushing with the grain. (**photo 1**) Allow to dry.

2. Working in the direction of the wood grain, rub a thin layer of petroleum jelly randomly in patches over piece, leaving some areas untouched. (**photo 2**) The petroleum jelly should be thin enough to see, but not thick and gooey. Let sit for about 1 hour to penetrate.

Can't find an old piece you like? The look of age on wood is easily to duplicate with paint, petroleum jelly, and sandpaper, even on new wood. Follow the easy steps below to create your own timeworn masterpiece.

3. Thin warm white (or other topcoat paint) with an equal amount of water. Using a bristle brush, apply a coat of paint over entire piece, following the grain of the wood. (**photo 3**) Note that the paint does not adhere to the areas where you applied the petroleum jelly.

4. Rinse brush and dry. Dip the brush in undiluted warm white paint.

Remove most of the paint from the brush by dabbing it off on a paper towel. (This is called a "dry brush.") Dry brush paint over the surface, Allow to dry several hours. Note that the areas coated with petroleum jelly continue to resist the paint and that the paint has started to bead up. (**photo 4**) Let dry.

Photo 1

Photo 2

Photo 3

5. Gently wipe areas where petroleum jelly was applied with soft paper towels, going with the grain of the wood. (**photo 5**) This gives the look of rubbed and chipping paint.

6. Sand the edges of the piece and other areas where the paint would naturally be worn with age. (**photo 6**) Wipe away sanding dust.

7. Apply an antiquing glaze randomly over the surface, concentrating the color in cracks and crevices. ❏

ABOVE: *The finished shelf looks as though it has been in the family for years. A few "old" accessories complete the look.*

Photo 4

Photo 5

Photo 6

BLUE & WHITE

Crisp and clean or soft and subdued, the various shades of blue evoke the tranquility of water and sky. The arrangement and selection of accessories and accents set the style and decorative tone of a room. For example, a blue room takes on the flavor of the sea with the addition of nautical items such as model ships and porthole-shaped mirrors. Combining red stripes, plaids, or shiny apples with slate blue connotes a folk art or patriotic style; checks, gingham, and ticking fabrics in blue and white have country cottage appeal. Sheer fabrics and wispy ruffles are romantic and relaxed. Regardless of your style preference, blue and white is pleasing to look at and creates a warm and comfortable environment.

One wonder of blue and white is how the unlimited variations of patterns and hues can be mixed and matched and displayed alongside each other. Chinese porcelains, accented with brilliant royal blue to subtle blues found in Delft or English patterns are lovely against many backgrounds – yellow, red, white, even lime green. Because of their availability and affordability, blue and white china and transferware are easy to collect, functional, and decorative.

PREVIOUS PAGE: *Blue and white china is just as beautiful when casually displayed in an old country pine cabinet as it is in a formal mahogany breakfront. Don't be afraid to use it regularly for serving meals or even quick snacks. Deep bowls or soup tureens can serve as colorful planters. (Try them for forcing bulbs around the holidays.) The dramatic contrast of blue and white with the color red makes filling bowls with apples an everyday favorite.*

RIGHT: *Pine floors painted with coats and coats of glossy white paint remind us of a gleaming boat deck. White painted walls and woodwork and nautical-themed accessories are a pleasing combination in this blue-and-white bedroom. Gingham fabrics, a rag rug, and wicker furniture completes the New England sea coast style.*

LEFT: *A collection of transferware is gathered on and around this mantel. Nails and plate hangers are used to attach lids and a plate to the wooden mantel. The colors of the china complement the colors of a painting by the homeowner.*

BELOW: *A wooden table was tailored so that a transferware platter would fit into a cutout in the table. The hole was cut slightly smaller than the platter so that the lip of the platter rests on the wood. Rather than sitting on top of the table, the platter fits into the table and becomes part of the table top. The platter is the perfect surface to use for holding potted plants or as a tray for serving drinks. The edge of the wood table was trimmed in blue to coordinate with the platter.*

MAKE-IT-YOURSELF

Covered Lampshade

SUPPLIES

Lamp base

Self-adhesive lampshade

Glue gun and glue sticks

Scissors

Fabric

Trim

Pencil

Self-adhesive lampshades make it easy to create a custom look. Here, a blue and white fabric makes a lovely shade for an old alabaster marble lamp base. The amount of fabric and trim you'll need is determined by the size of the shade. Remember to select the right size shade for the size of your base.

If you like, you can purchase a lamp wiring kit at the hardware store and create your own lamp base. (Try an old baluster with chipping white paint.) A lighting shop can make just about anything into a lamp if you don't want to do it yourself.

Photo 1

Photo 2

Photo 3

Photo 4

INSTRUCTIONS

1. Remove the paper protector from the shade and use it as your pattern. Lay out fabric right-side-up and place paper pattern on top. Use a pencil to trace around the pattern, adding 1" all around for seam allowances. (**photos 1 & 2**)

2. Cut out fabric according to pattern. (**photo 3**)

Photo 5

Photo 6

3. Position fabric on shade, with right side of fabric on outside of shade with 1" extending at top and bottom. (**photo** 4) Hand press fabric to shade, smoothing side to side and top to bottom. Reposition as needed to eliminate ripples. Trim seam allowances to 3/8".

4. Glue back seam edge to shade with hot glue. Clip top seam allowance every 1/2". Glue top and bottom seam allowances to inside of the shade, rolling fabric snugly over wired edge. (**photo 5**)

5. Glue trim to top and bottom edges, starting and stopping at the back seam. *Option:* Use trim to cover unfinished edges inside shade. ❏

I still remember my first flea market purchase – an exquisite, but inexpensive, blue and white bowl. With global roots extending from China to England, the many themes and patterns of blue and white china offer classic appeal. From the popular Blue Willow pattern to Flowblue, the color varies with the age of the piece – typically, the older the piece, the more subdued the color; however, new reproductions now mimic the aged appearance.

The presence of hairline cracks (called "crazing") help determine age. (To intensify the appearance of crazing, soak china or transferware in a tea bath: Use 2 tea bags in 8 oz. of water and soak overnight.

Rinse with cool water and dry.)

Anchored by an antique mahogany drop leaf table, *below,* a collection of blue and white plates, platters, and lids from serving dishes adds color, dimension, and interest to this entryway when hung in a symmetrical arrangement around an arched-top framed mirror.

The painted yellow kitchen cupboard, *right,* houses a collection of pitchers, platters, and plates. Small hooks screwed into the edge of one shelf are used to display cups. Yellow adds a bright accent to the blue and white color scheme.

ABOVE: *This very simple arrangement shows how to achieve a sleek look with clean lines using blue and white. Notice the absence of a color except for the blue details on the porcelain lamp and natural tones of the seashell collection. White wicker and pottery add interesting texture against white shutters and window.*

RIGHT: *A touch of blue is found on this otherwise all-white room. The country fresh bedroom is furnished with flea market finds, painted white for a coordinated look. Note the variety of interesting shapes, such as the bedside pedestal table's scalloped trim and the arched, ornamented headboard.*

RED & WHITE

When you think of red, do you think of power, strength, or passion? The color red symbolizes all of these qualities, but red also can be soft, gentle, mild, and romantic. Used in home decor, red reacts beautifully with other colors and invigorates the eye. Red accents add dramatic interest to a room, and red is a perfect background for displaying collections.

Found in vintage style fabrics, china, watering cans, and tins, red and white collectibles are compatible with a range of decorating styles. A French look is achieved when red and white items are combined with painted iron and ornamental accessories. Using red and white to create a cottage look is easy and a favorite of mine – mixing large scale red and white floral fabrics with stripes and plaids and using red accents of different textures throughout a room further define the style.

RIGHT: *Red and white transferware looks great in a whitewashed pine nook. The mirror intensifies the effect of the red flowers.*

A room full of texture and pattern is a delight for the eye. In this dining room, *left,* chairs slipcovered in a small scale red and white floral fabric surround a French provincial table. Natural light cascades through the draped windows, while special lamps, candles, and a hanging crystal chandelier add soft illumination.

A discarded fireplace mantel, also seen in a closeup *below,* is used as a piece of furniture. A small table placed where the firebox would be holds a red-painted wedding chest. The chest is used for storage; wedding china is stacked on top of it. The mantel shelf displays an arrangement of shapely objects.

The multitude of red and white objects in this fanciful setting, *right,* creates a comfortable and relaxed atmosphere. An oak pedestal table is painted white and set with red and white china for an afternoon tea. Chairs slipcovered in red and white striped ticking are colorful and practical.

A red-painted wooden stepladder, *right and below,* displays a collection of white pitchers. Crisp white linen vintage handkerchiefs, placed diagonally, soften and dress up the steps.

The photographs on these two pages are closeups of the setting on the previous pages. Notice how the red berry sprays in the alabaster centerpiece and the miniature apples on the plates provide colorful accents for the china. Greenery, berries, and fruit are appropriate accents for flowery motifs.

Placing the pitchers with their spouts facing the same way and grouping them on the steps by size adds a touch of formality to an otherwise casual arrangement.

ABOVE: *Keeping your collections accessible makes it easy to use and enjoy them. This opening above the kitchen stove was designed to hold spices, but it makes a convenient display space for a collection of pitchers and red and white transferware.*

RIGHT: *Softly muted red and white fabrics are restful and energizing. Natural wood floors, trim, and wainscoting and lots of white balance the multitude of prints, checks, and stripes on pillows and upholstery. Bright red accents come in the bowl of apples on the table, the red flowers, and the metal watering can.*

Less-than-perfect vintage linens and tablecloths can be recycled into one-of-a-kind pillows. Stained or torn tablecloths are perfect candidates for sewing projects, and they are less expensive than ones in perfect condition.

RIGHT: *Outdoor items come indoors. Red and white pillows soften an old wooden lawn chair; a slate blue wheelbarrow works as a coffee table. A blue and white enameled bowl holds apples; a white watering can graces the red brick hearth.*

BELOW: *Color provides the basis for this collection of tins and patterned china. Stylized cherries, checkerboards, and flowers have timeless appeal. Tins make great storage containers, too.*

Muted blues help cool and balance fiery reds. The blue-painted finishes on the turned-leg wooden table and simple stool, *left,* show years of age and weathering. The tabletop has been sanded clean to reveal the wood underneath; the apron and legs of the table and the stool were sanded just enough to create a smooth surface and reveal layers of color. The bright red tin bin once held coffee.

An old pie safe, *below,* is topped with a blue-painted toolbox that holds a collection of pie-making items and bright vintage linens. The lamp, made from a pottery jug, sports a red shade with ruffled trim and is positioned to illuminate the framed cross-stitch sampler on the wall.

BLACK ACCENTS

Compatible with any style of decor, black accents can evoke elegance, country charm, or a sense of antiquity. Used in moderation, black adds balance and impact; it is amazing how quickly a room is dressed by embellishing it with touches of black. Black marble candlesticks, wrought iron details, picture frames, books, and fabrics are some of the ways that this striking color is incorporated in a room.

Combined with other colors, black can be bold and classic or rich and regal. Black and white make a bold, graphic statement. Black absorbs light, while white reflects it – together, they create movement and excitement. Especially popular on floors, black and white checkerboard patterns are used in many different kinds of settings and work to anchor the room for the addition of other colors and tones. The boldness of black and white can be softened with a brown antiquing glaze, changing the feel from classic elegance to rustic country cottage.

With warm red tones, black accents are rich and stylish. Perfect for a dining area or a man's study, this combination is cozy and inviting. For a classic touch, add prints or engravings of hunt scenes or dog breeds.

Black collectibles, including small furniture, lamps, frames, and ironwork, stand out against light backgrounds.

RIGHT: *A black and white tile floor is a classic look, extended by the drapery fabric, the framed art, and the upholstered seats of the chairs. The bold color of the painted table provides balance.*

A black and white floor is also a classic bathroom look, *right*. The owners kept the original wooden cabinetry, cleaning layers of paint from the vintage hardware, and adding recycled beadboard wainscoting on the walls. Color comes from the ruffled pillow on the black-painted bentwood chair, the shower curtain, and a vase of palm fronds and flowers, *below*. Shiny chrome and silver accents – found on the light fixtures, faucets, a silver tray, and candelabra – are cool against white.

The wonderful black mantel is the elegant focal point in this comfortable, restful room. It's the perfect place in any season for an afternoon nap or for curling up with a good book.

Black paint can revive and transform wooden chests, chairs, and tables. Look around at what you already have or shop flea markets for well-made pieces. Sand the surface smooth and apply a few coats of black paint in an eggshell finish. For a distressed look, sand to expose the natural wood or other paint color(s) underneath. Add vintage hardware for an heirloom look.

This sleek black-painted chest, left, provides a surface for display and more storage space than a table.

A new table, *right,* was painted white and edged and stenciled with black to resemble the porcelain-topped kitchen tables of the 1920s and 30s. Paired with old chairs, freshly painted and reupholstered in black and white checks, the set looks right at home on the black and white tile floor. On the table, a woven mat is the foundation for a colorful display. The neutral-colored basketweave-pattern pottery vase holds a simple arrangement of twigs and leafy grapevines that softens the starkness of the black and white. The vase's color is echoed in the pillar candles that top black-painted iron candlesticks. Harvest vegetables, berries, and leaves provide color.

COLORS OF THE GARDEN

The natural colors of the earth, grass, and flowers remind us of the peacefulness of the outdoors. Decorating with the colors of the garden presents a splendid opportunity to reflect nature's beauty and bring the outdoors in.

The color choices are many. You can opt for the soft, faded floral patterns and colors of vintage prints or choose vivid, bold hues in tropical motifs. Found in the foliage of almost all plants, green is a neutral in the garden and in garden-themed decorating that evokes serenity and tranquility.

Try bringing outdoor objects like birdhouses, baskets, garden tools, watering cans, wheelbarrows, wrought iron, fence posts, and moss-covered pots indoors to extend the garden theme.

And don't forget to fill your room with fresh flowers and thriving plants in interesting containers. Ivy is beautiful when draped over furniture or tucked in a nook. Ferns soften and fill corners of a room and look nice atop old columns or on iron plant stands.

RIGHT: *The brick floor adds a rough outdoor texture to this sunroom. The rustic wooden coffee table is topped with wooden-handled garden tools and a galvanized tin container that holds leafy geraniums. A tiny birdhouse and a squirrel statue complete the arrangement. A small painted wheelbarrow under the table can hold magazines or newspapers. Floral patterned pillows adorn a white-slipcovered sofa.*

76

In this guest bedroom, French toile fabric on the upholstered headboard and bedskirt is unexpectedly paired with a floral-motif quilt atop a matelasse coverlet. A pair of pillows, one with a teapot, the other a teacup, draws the eye to the teapot collection on a butler's tray in the corner of the room and *below*. The floral-motif china plates hung on the wall above the headboard echo the print fabric in the quilt.

The teapot collection is illuminated by a lamp with an urn-style china base in coordinating colors.

The beadboard walls and ceiling of this bedroom are painted a soft teal reminiscent of the color used on porch ceilings in the 1930s and 40s. The color is relieved with white – a white bedspread, white trim, white night tables, white lampshades – and reinforced by the background of the pieced quilt on the bed. A picket fence remnant with peeling white paint serves as a headboard. Two antique wooden garden rakes are hung on the wall above the bed around a window frame painted with a planter of daffodils. Reverse painting on glass turns the frame into a work of art. See how to make one like it on the pages that follow.

MAKE-IT-YOURSELF

Painted Window Frame

Designed by Alyson Tucker

Blooming flowers last all year long when painted on a salvaged window-pane. For the painting, choose acrylic paints intended for painting on glass, which are available at crafts stores.

SUPPLIES

Old window frame with glass

Painter's masking tape

Window cleaner

Paper towels

Disposable palette

Acrylic enamel or gloss paints suitable for painting on glass: White, lavender, red, green, yellow, brown, blue, terra cotta, black, crown gold

Artist's paint brushes

Optional: Crackle medium, foam or bristle paint brush

INSTRUCTIONS

Frame:

If you like the way your window frame looks, you can clean the frame and sand lightly to smooth any flaking or chipping paint. To change the color and create an aged look, follow these steps:

1. Tape off inside of each windowpane with low tack painter's masking tape.

2. Paint frame with white. Let dry.

3. Apply crackle medium according to manufacturer's instructions.

4. Brush red paint over the crackle medium. Cracks will appear. Let dry. Remove tape.

Painting on Glass:

1. Clean both sides of the glass with window cleaner, making sure to remove any tape residue.

2. Enlarge pattern as needed to fit your window. Cut pattern apart to accommodate the panes of your window. Place the pattern pieces on the back side of the glass so the pattern shows through on the front side of the glass.

3. Squeeze paint colors on a palette. Basecoat the design elements with the pattern taped in place, using the photo as a guide for placement of colors, or using colors of your choice.

   • Depending on the color, basecoating may require multiple coats until solid coverage is accomplished.
   • Allow paint to dry 2-4 hours between coats.
   • After basecoating, you will no longer be able to see the pattern.

4. Using the photo as a guide, paint details and add highlights and shading. Let dry at least 48 hours.

5. Clean away any fingerprints with a paper towel moistened with glass cleaner. ❏

Pattern for Garden Window

Enlarge to fit your window frame.

Join at center to complete pattern.

Called "the queen of flowers," roses – in hues of mauve, pink, yellow, and red – recall the beauty of an old-fashioned garden. For centuries, the rose has been a popular motif for fabrics, china, porcelains, and prints. Rose patterns in all styles, shapes, and tints are fun to collect. Other popular flowers include violets and pansies; all add color and beauty.

A collection of floral-themed china platters, plates, tea cups, teapots, creamers, and sugar bowls are carefully arranged in and around a pine wall shelf, *right.* The framed teapot prints above the shelf echo the display.

A closeup view of one shelf, *below,* shows how plates are arranged in layers. Floral-patterned chintzware cups and saucers are arranged in front of the plates.

An ornate wooden table with spindle trim, painted a soft green color, flanks one side of the bed in this room, *left.* The round doily under the lamp echoes the shape of the lamp base and floral print leaning against the wall. A cast metal doorstop in the shape of a bouquet, its colors still bright, is elevated to tabletop height. The floral-patterned hatbox on the table shelf provides storage. A basket beside the table holds pillows made from quilt fragments.

Memories of grandmother's home flourish in this bedroom, where a small antique quilt, *opposite page,* is hung as a canopy over an iron and brass bed. The Mosaic pattern of this quilt is considered the "grandmother" of the more modern Grandmother's Flower Garden pattern. The blocks of the quilt on the bed, separated with rectangles of pink, are a pattern called Hands-All-Around.

A white watering can and a tall weathered wood birdhouse embellished with an architectural spindle and old tin ceiling tiles are garden-inspired accents on the bedside table.

LEFT: *Colors of the garden come to the kitchen counter. An English platter with a floral border, a chintz-patterned china teapot, and two pottery bowls are parts of a harmonious, colorful display. The white bowl is Roseville; the green one is McCoy.*

BELOW: *Even small accessories can extend a theme. Here, the handpainted floral garland below the clock face is an inspired choice for a garden-theme room.*

An old linen and lace tablecloth is hung behind a bed, *right,* to soften the wooden wall. The mound of colorful floral-patterned pillows in gently faded pinks and reds look inviting. The bright red train case adds a hit of intense color and coordinates with the ticking stripes of the turned-back covers.

A miniature dresser that once graced a doll's bedroom, *below,* provides drawer space for a bedside table that has none and elevates a pot of tulips.

A mix of old and new small-scale floral print fabrics in coordinating soft colors are combined in this bedroom, *left,* on an assortment of pillows, the bed coverings, a slipcovered chair, and a ruffled and pleated lampshade on a floor lamp. A painted metal chandelier suspended above the bed is a whimsical touch.

Part of an antique vanity, *below,* elevated by bed linens, rests on a wooden stool, providing storage and a surface for display.

Handpainted Austrian vases glow with pearly luster, *right,* in front of a gold-framed mirror that reflects their beauty. The colors of the flowers in the bouquet of lilies in the pitcher echo the colors of the roses on the vases.

A collection of silver-backed bristle brushes nestle in a container on a dresser tray, *below,* with a bracelet collection arranged on a mannequin's arm. A floral-trimmed brush and mirror set rest on a linen dresser scarf trimmed with tatted lace.

THE MELLOW PATINA OF AGING

s I get older, I like to think of myself as mellowing, rather than aging. The same holds true for furniture pieces and accessories that show the gentle wear and mellowing of age. We are drawn to furniture and accent pieces that exhibit these qualities perhaps because they reflect the reality in us.

When I was preparing to write this book, I consulted my good friend Eileen Cannon Paulin, editor of *Romantic Homes* magazine. Eileen recognizes the appeal and charm of decorating with fine antiques as well as flea market finds and collections, and she and her staff capture casual elegance and personal style in the many homes they feature each month.

With her artful eye, Eileen pointed me to many of the homes featured in this book and agreed to contribute her insights. Here she shares some of her suggestions and experiences for achieving the romantic look through the mellow patina of aging.

RIGHT: *A pair of teal and sea blue shutters with sailboat cutouts that show years of wear are the perfect wall decoration for this seaside cottage. Hung side by side on a wood plank wall, they add a splash of color.*

98

Words from Eileen

Everything is richer and more interesting when it has history, and home furnishings are no exception. Gracefully aged furniture and accessories contribute a casual elegance to any home. Their warmth and comfort are unsurpassed by any new showroom piece. Joyfully, you don't need the fortunate luck of inheriting rooms full of furniture or an infinite amount of money to enjoy this wonderfully romantic look. Rejoice in the pieces that may have been handed down to you, then fill in with finds from expeditions to antique and consignment stores and flea markets.

Delight in finding new uses for old items. A small section of vintage picket fencing can be a great fireplace screen for the summer months. Weathered balcony balusters make terrific candleholders on a mantel. Old shutters hung on a wall add instant age and give a room architectural appeal. A farm bench makes a delightful coffee table, and an old phonograph cabinet makes a wonderful buffet or silver storage chest. A salvaged leaded-glass window hung inside the frame of a new window brings ambiance to a room when it plays with the sunlight streaming in. Add furniture legs, and a window can be used as a table. Interesting old suitcases have many uses; think about fitting a deep one to serve as file storage for your home office. A vintage lace tablecloth makes an exquisite bed canopy, its beauty unsurpassed.

Gently aged items bring instant history into any home. It's always intriguing to think about where enchanting items have been and who owned them before us. I have a great deal of fun dreaming up imaginary stories for some of my favorite treasures. One day while shopping at an antique mall with a dear friend, we were delighted to discover the real story behind a cache of hand-painted china we found. Captivated by the beauty of the artist's work, we looked closely to see each piece was signed "Isabelle Radic." The store manager had purchased the pieces from her heirs and was able to tell us that Isabelle and her husband had lived in New York City where they led what sounded like a fashionable metropolitan life. Somewhere along the line, they opted for rural living and moved to Iowa to farm and raise hogs. Isabelle passed the time painting china. We carefully chose several pieces, and marveled all the way home about the fading art and the days when women had time for such pursuits. Later that night, my friend raised her glass in a toast "To Isabelle," whose china adds a special adopted history to the mantel in my living room.

Don't let some of the popular trends in romantic decorating fool you into thinking that old has to mean peeling, cracking, or falling apart. The mellow patina of aging suggests that the object was lovely and of good quality to begin with. It has aged gracefully, with a gentle timeworn dignity. There is a beauty and a kind of wisdom in the age of these treasures — what more could we hope for our homes and ourselves!

Eileen Cannon Paulin

LEFT: *You can almost hear the roar of the ocean lapping against the sand in this sea green bedroom. The chipped painted finish of the old writing table contrasts with the newly upholstered chair. A lamp base made from local driftwood, a picture of the dunes supported by an artful stack of books, and a small arrangement of seashells remind us of the seaside.*

BELOW: *An antique painted chest, softly yellowed with age, greets guests in the entry of this cottage home. A classical-themed arrangement of obviously, but gently worn objects is stacked and layered to make an interesting, eye-catching display. A golden angel flies above the framed mirror.*

LEFT: *Fabrics billow and gather, turning this bedroom into a dreamy retreat. The large expanses of neutral tones balance the deep pink of the curtains behind the bed, the small rectangular pillow, and the child's dress hung from the curtain rod. The faded floral fabrics of the pillows incorporate all the room's colors.*

ABOVE: *An antique dropleaf table with a Hepplewhite-style drawer pull displays an old pair of brass binoculars resting on a stack of books, a pair of stenciled wooden trunks, and a round shaving mirror on a swivel stand.*

A curvy upholstered sofa, *right,* is adorned with vintage pillows and draped with lacy fringed shawls. A simple, narrow bench is used as a coffee table. A hooked wool rug echoes the soft colors. A basket under the bench holds books and magazines; an old ironstone bowl on top holds pomegranates.

This old train case size piece of luggage with scuffed red faux alligator trim, *below,* is the perfect storage place for a selection of colorful paper napkins. Inside the lid, a whimsical print in bright colors is held in place by clips that once held a mirror.

MAKE-IT-YOURSELF

Tea Dyeing

SUPPLIES

Natural-fiber fabric

Tea bags

Hot water (about 4 cups for each yard of fabric)

Container (large enough to hold the tea bath and the fabric)

Dishwashing liquid

INSTRUCTIONS

Prepare Tea Bath:

1. Boil water. Add tea bags. (I use 2 family-size tea bags for 10 cups of water. About 4 regular (individual) tea bags = 1 family size tea bag. Additional tea bags can be added for a darker color.)

2. Allow tea to steep. Remove bags and let cool. Transfer water to the container for the tea bath.

Prepare & Dye Fabric:

1. Wet fabric to be dyed until thoroughly saturated. Wring out.

2. Place wet fabric in tea bath. Stir to evenly distribute material, making sure the tea gets in the folds of the fabric. (**photo 1**) Let soak until the color pleases you. The longer the fabric soaks, the darker the color will be. After about 30 minutes, fabric should be a light tan color.

Dyeing fabric with tea is an easy way to create an antique look or disguise a stain on a favorite piece of linen. It's just as simple as it sounds: Fabric is soaked in a bath of tea until the desired color is achieved. Natural fabrics such as cotton, linen, and wool work best – their fibers absorb the pigment in the tea leaving them with a faint sepia tone. (Polyesters and other synthetics, which repel liquid, do not work well.) Try this technique on napkins, tablecloths, sheets, pillowcases, lace, trim, ribbon, handkerchiefs, printed fabrics, and even silk flowers.

3. Remove fabric. (**photo 2**) Rinse under warm water to which you have added a little dishwashing liquid. (This removes the tannic acid from the fabric and keeps it from weakening over time.)

4. Hang fabric to dry.

5. Iron to heat set.

TIPS & OPTIONS

• If tea-dyed fabric is too dark, wash it with a small amount of bleach to lighten.

• For a darker color, use coffee. Brew a strong pot of coffee, cool and transfer to container. Follow the steps for tea dyeing; soaking time will likely be shorter.

• To create a faded look, follow same instructions but substitute bleach for tea. Use 1 part bleach to 1 part water and soak fabric until sufficiently faded. ❏

Photo 1

Photo 2

MAKE-IT-YOURSELF

Tea-Dyed Pillow with Silk Roses

This beautiful pillow, made from all new materials, duplicates the romantic elegance of a Victorian-era antique. Special thanks to my son Wesley, who helped me with this project.

SUPPLIES

White cutwork dishtowel (14" x 22")

Needle

Off-white thread

Polyester pillow stuffing

7 white silk roses, stems removed

Glue gun and glue sticks

1 yd. ecru satin ribbon (you may tea dye white satin ribbon)

INSTRUCTIONS

1. Tea dye fabric and silk roses, following instructions above and soaking fabric until desired color is achieved. (Silk roses may need to be soaked overnight.)
2. Remove all from tea bath and allow to dry thoroughly.
3. Press fabric.
4. Fold hand towel in half, right sides together, allowing cutwork to overhang one edge.
5. Sew side seams together. Turn right side out.
6. Stuff pillow. Hand stitch the opening at bottom to form a pillow.
7. Hot glue rose blossoms on pillow side by side as shown.
8. Tie ribbon in a bow. Hot glue underneath roses. ❑

RIGHT: *Examples of tea-dyed fabrics and trims.*

ABOVE: *An iron headboard, painted to resemble the color copper turns with age, is the colorful anchor in this bedroom. A gently aged shuttered wall cabinet makes an unusual but effective wall decoration on the wood-paneled wall. Small framed prints are propped on top.*

RIGHT: *The dark wood tones of the furniture in this entry are reminiscent of a rustic country cottage. The portrait of the dogs has the same brown tones as the Windsor chair and old farm table. A stair-stepped holder displays a collection of old wooden spoons. The wooden bread bowl can hold mail or fruit. A china saucer collects keys.*

MAKE-IT-YOURSELF

Distressing (or Antiquing) Unfinished Wood

SUPPLIES

A new wooden item

Hammer, saw, nails, chain, or other tools to distress the wood

Acrylic craft paint, one or more colors of your choice (We used barn red and off white.)

Wax (white candles work well)

Paint brushes

Paint scraper

Sandpaper, 220 grit

Antiquing glaze

Sponge

Optional: Old toothbrush

INSTRUCTIONS

1. Using a hammer, nails, or other items, create dents, small holes, and signs of wear on the wood surface. (**photo 1**)
2. Apply wax to surface with the grain of the wood, concentrating in areas where paint would most likely be worn away by handling, such as edges. (**photo 2**)
3. *Option:* If you don't want the wood to show, apply 1-3 coats of the base color and let dry (**photo 3**). Then apply the wax.
4. Apply 1-3 coats of paint. (**photo 4**) The paint coats can be the same color or different colors. Let dry between coats, but do not sand between coats. For a layered effect, use two or more paint colors. Allow paint to dry between colors and rub the wax over the painted surface before adding the next color. When scraped and sanded, all colors will show.
5. Scrape surface with paint scraper working in the direction of the wood grain to reveal the raw wood or base

A distressed or antique look is easy to create with paint and antiquing glaze. The same technique can be used to create a worn look on any new wooden item; we used an unfinished stool purchased at a crafts store.

Be sure to use clear or white candle or canning wax (paraffin), sold at grocery and hardware stores Do not use colored candles – the candle dye could stain the wood.

paint or both. (**photo 5**) In areas where wax was applied, paint will flake off easily. Brush away excess paint particles.
6. Sand surface to smooth areas where

paint was removed.
7. Apply an antiquing glaze with a sponge, rubbing in the direction of the wood grain to mellow the effect and soften the paint colors.

Photo 1

Photo 2

8. *Option:* Mix 1 part antiquing glaze with 2 parts water. Dip an old toothbrush in the mixture and spatter paint on the piece by running your finger across the brush bristles. ❏

ABOVE: *An unfinished wooden stool takes on the look of a discovered treasure. Barn red paint was used for the basecoat. Wax was applied. Off white paint was used as a topcoat. Scraping, sanding, and antiquing followed.*

Photo 3

Photo 4

Photo 5

RICH
METALLICS

Through the ages, gold and silver have symbolized richness, wealth, luxury, and prosperity. The shimmering sparkle and shine of metallics add old world elegance to new world style. Rich metallic accents are like jewelry – they catch the eye.

Metallics are bright and glimmering, and catch your eye with their beauty. For a more mellow look, metallics can be allowed to age. Copper, bronze and even silver, allowed to wear their patina, have character and stability. Decorative accessories such as frames, clocks, trays, tea service pieces, candlesticks add richness to any décor.

Mirrors add light, dimension, and reflection. Grouped together, *shown right*, mirrors of different sizes and shapes make an interesting display. To determine how to hang a grouping, trace the shapes of the mirrors on brown kraft paper. Cut out the shapes and position them on the wall with low-tack masking tape, re-arranging until you find an arrangement that suits you. Then mark the wall and hang. Mirrors can be heavy – be sure to choose hangers that will accommodate their weight.

RIGHT: *Polished silver and brass candlesticks gleam on a mantel; placing them in front of a mirror magnifies their impact. Old teapots and coffee pots can hold flowers or be transformed, with the addition of a wiring kit, into interesting lamp bases like this one. The white drum shade is wrapped with a vintage remnant of embroidery on tulle and edged with lace.*

RIGHT: *Grouped together, the shapes, details, and shine of metal candlesticks and picture frames make an interesting tabletop display. Cut-glass prisms reflect light and add sparkle. Dried flowers, neutral-toned candles, and a wicker tray are natural touches.*

Mirrors are easy to locate at flea markets and antique stores; the price depends greatly on the type and condition of the frame that surrounds it. Generally, the more decorative and intricate the frame, the more expensive the mirror. An economical approach is to have a glass shop cut a mirror to fit an old frame. To age a new mirror, scrape off some of the backing with a pumice stone or razor blade and rub the scraped areas lightly with black shoe polish or oil.

When placing a mirror, pay attention to what it reflects, as it will emphasize (and reveal the back of) anything you place in front of it.

A myriad of mirrors, *right,* makes up the unusual treatment on and above this fireplace mantel. The angular edges of the mantel are softened with vintage fabrics. Candlestick lamps with fringed shades cast a warm glow.

BELOW: *Metallic accessories dress up the rustic wooden walls in this bedroom. The metal lamp base, silver pitcher filled with flowers, and a gold-rimmed plate are arranged in front of an antique mirror. Classic-theme porcelains in ornate frames hang above the mirror.*

RIGHT: *Sometimes not polishing is best! The metal base and filigree shade of the lamp have been darkened by time. The two silver pitchers wear their tarnish proudly. The neck of the pitcher on the left is draped with an antique watch pendant framed with a silver horseshoe.*

ABOVE: *The lacy gold patterns on the Czechoslovakian wedding china and the small rectangular dish are complemented by the pattern of the sheer lace on the box under the pitcher. Elevating some pieces in a collection on plate stands or boxes makes all the pieces visible.*

French influences and classical motifs are evident in this formal arrangement, *right,* on a painted sideboard. The repetition of round shapes – the sconce mirrors, clock faces, even the wreath on the lamp base – are a designer's dream. The crystal lamp finial echoes the crystals of the chandelier seen in the mirror.

Below, a polished silver vase filled with a simple arrangement of white roses makes a lovely accent on a mantel.

MAKE-IT-YOURSELF

Framed Aged Finish Mirrors
"Mirror" with Gold Leafed Frame

SUPPLIES

Wooden picture frame with glass

Glass cleaner

Paper towels

400 wet/dry sandpaper or 0000 steel wool

Acrylic craft paint - Deep red, black

Gold leaf

Silver leaf

Leaf adhesive

Leaf sealer

Small flat bristle brush

Cardboard

Cotton swab

Warm, soapy water

Optional: Neutral glazing medium

The rich look of gilding is created by applying micro-thin sheets of composition metal called "leaf" to surfaces such as metal, wood, glass, or paper. Thanks to modern manufacturing techniques, a process once considered difficult and expensive has become easy and affordable. Leafing is a simple way to create a rich-looking accessory from a flea market find. Silver leafing, applied to the back of a piece of glass, gives the look of an antique mirror. Before you begin, protect your work surface with paper to catch the small flecks of leafing.

INSTRUCTIONS

Glass:

1. Thoroughly clean the glass with glass cleaner. Wipe dry.

2. Brush leaf adhesive on one side of the glass, using even, consistent strokes. (**photo 1**) Let adhesive set until tacky (usually 30-60 minutes).

3. Carefully place a sheet of silver leaf over the tacky adhesive on the glass. (**photo 2**). Gently smooth with a dry brush. (**photo 3**) Continue applying silver leaf until glass is covered.

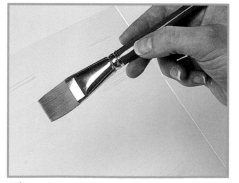

Photo 1

Photo 2

Photo 3

- As you apply the leaf, it will wrinkle and overlap.
- As you press down and lightly brush, excess leaf will be removed.
- Do not worry about slight tears or areas that are not covered – that adds to the look of old mirror.
- For additional aged appearance, dip a cotton swab in warm, soapy water and rub off some of the silver leaf, using a circular motion.

4. Gently brush a coat of black acrylic paint over the silver leaf on the glass. (**photo** 4) This will fill in any gaps between pieces of leaf, giving the look of an old, worn mirror. Allow to dry.

Frame:

1. Clean and lightly sand wooden frame. Remove dust with a tack cloth or dampened paper towel.

2. Paint wood frame with deep red paint. (**photo** 5) Allow to dry.

3. Brush a thin coat of gold leaf adhesive on the frame, using even, consistent strokes. Let adhesive set until tacky (usually 30-60 minutes).

4. Carefully place a sheet of gold leaf over the tacky adhesive on the frame. (**photo** 6). Gently smooth with a dry brush. Continue applying silver leaf until glass is covered.

5. When complete, spray frame with leaf sealer.

6. *Option:* To tone down the shininess of the gold leaf, mix 1 part black paint with 2 parts neutral glazing medium. Brush over gold leafing. (**photo** 7) Let dry.

continued on next page

Photo 4

Photo 5

Photo 6

MAKE-IT-YOURSELF

continued from page 125

Assembly:
Secure mirror in frame with the clean side of the glass facing out. (**photo 8**) ❑

Photo 7   *Photo 8*

"Mirror" with Black Frame

SUPPLIES

Ornate wooden picture frame with glass

Fine sandpaper

Tack cloth

Black spray paint, satin sheen

Optional: Silver buffing cream, soft cloth

INSTRUCTIONS

Glass:
Apply silver to one side of the glass, following the instructions above.

Frame:

1. Lightly sand surface of frame. Wipe away dust with a tack cloth.

2. Spray with black paint. Let dry.

3. *Option:* To add a metallic gleam, rub silver buffing cream over frame to highlight and bring out details. Buff with a soft cloth.

Assembly:
Secure mirror in frame with clean side of the glass facing out. ❑

Metric Conversion Chart

Inches to Millimeters and Centimeters

Inches	MM	CM
1/8	3	.3
1/4	6	.6
3/8	10	1.0
1/2	13	1.3
5/8	16	1.6
3/4	19	1.9
7/8	22	2.2
1	25	2.5
1-1/4	32	3.2
1-1/2	38	3.8
1-3/4	44	4.4
2	51	5.1
3	76	7.6
4	102	10.2
5	127	12.7
6	152	15.2
7	178	17.8
8	203	20.3
9	229	22.9
10	254	25.4
11	279	27.9
12	305	30.5

Yards to Meters

Yards	Meters
1/8	.11
1/4	.23
3/8	.34
1/2	.46
5/8	.57
3/4	.69
7/8	.80
1	.91
2	1.83
3	2.74
4	3.66
5	4.57
6	5.49
7	6.40
8	7.32
9	8.23
10	9.14

Index